A GUIDE TO

RABBIT-PROOF GARDENING

FIFTH EDITION

Published
October 2002

Printed in Glasgow

CONTENTS

page

INTRODUCTION

I began writing this book in the hope my lessons of the last few years together with advice from gardening experts might make life easier for others pestered by unwelcome rabbits. Assuming that this problem can be addressed by simple experiment, I decided to treat my long-eared visitors to a feast of surprise menus. Little did I know just how many possibilites awaited discovery and how much was still to be learned.

When my first attempts to outwit our furry friend proved unsuccessful, I began to suspect he just likes things which either cost money or look beautiful and so the best idea would be to down tools and concentrate on creating a luscious lawn. However, the more I asked around, the more it became obvious that not everyone was stumped for answers, even though many gardeners admitted to simply fencing in their blooms or shooting the enemy!

To my surprise, the answer to the problem was different almost every time I asked: most experts seemed to have discovered a few plants of their own, but rarely did they recommend the same ones as their colleagues.

Possibilities suddenly began to open up. Could someone really create a varied display of plants without the need to fence them in? After all the frustration and seeming waste of time and energy, was there light at the end of the tunnel? Was the fight over? Was it too much to hope that gardener and enemy could occupy the same territory in peace?

Janet Thomson
November, 1996

1

FOREWORD

Rabbits. *Those cuddly, lovable creatures who are at their happiest crunching a chunk of carrot (or so writers of children's stories would have us believe)*

Rabbits. *Those lovely doe-eyed, docile, easy-to-look-after, economic-to-feed children's pets. They'll be happy chewing on a lettuce leaf (so pet shops would like us to believe).*

Rabbits. *Those quick-moving, burrowing, ever-hungry animals who can decimate a garden in a very short time, devouring all our favourite plants (as many gardeners have found to their cost).*
In other words:
THE GARDENER'S ENEMY.

Even pet rabbits, if they get out of their hutch, will rapidly devastate a garden. It is very difficult to discourage them once they have visited and discovered your plants: their food source!

Surrounding your garden with wire mesh which is dug down a couple of feet is one way to discourage them. But it won't be long until someone leaves your gate open and they slip back in.

Having worked with plants for many years and been asked for advice over and over again by customers, I have come to the conclusion that choosing plants which rabbits dislike is the best way to deal with this problem.

Alyson Dorrington

P.S. Rabbit droppings are an excellent source of garden manure!

THE RABBIT

The rabbit has a charming face:
Its private life is a disgrace.
I really dare not name to you
The awful things that rabbits do;
Things that your paper never prints -
You only mention them in hints.
They have such lost, degraded souls
No wonder they inhabit holes;
When such depravity is found
It only can live underground.

NAOMI ROYDE SMITH

Dedicated to the memory of the unknown rabbit:

the rabbit who ate no flowers.

1.
A POTTED HISTORY OF THE RABBIT

Most people love rabbits. Most gardeners harbour a secret soft spot for them yet all the while hate the sight of them. If you have bought this book, you will not need reminding of this feeling. But is it only gardeners who feel ambivalent towards the rabbit?

RABBIT

Order: *Lagomorpha*
Family: *Lepidorae*

These animals are also a pest to farmers, destroying trees and crops. However, few farmers could have remained unmoved on seeing a rabbit infected with myxomatosis. This virus, specific to rabbits, was introduced to devastating effect in Australia in 1951. The disease spread to Europe, resulting in blindness, disorientation and eventual death of huge numbers of rabbits.

Less well-known is the outbreak of viral haemorrhagic disease which has swept from the South of England to the North of Scotland in the last few years. Although a vaccine has been developed, the origin and means of transmission are unknown. Early attempts to control its spread failed and it is no longer a notifiable disease. Once infected, deterioration in health is rapid and the rabbit dies hidden away in its burrow or, more likely nowadays, in undergrowth. No-one could wish such a fate on his worst enemy, let alone on our own well-loved 'Brer

Recent history exploited people's attitude to rabbits when the song *"Run rabbit, run rabbit; run, run, run"* was aired as a jibe at the 'enemy'. This enemy may not be liked, but he is hardly feared for all that. Wartime children sang an evangelical chorus from the 1930's which ran:

> *"Root them out, get them gone:*
> *All the little rabbits in the field of corn.*
> *ENVY, JEALOUSY, MALICE, PRIDE:*
> *They must never in my heart abide."*

Written by adults for children, this song also chose the unthreatening image of the rabbit to illustrate undesirable sentiments to be 'rooted out'.

Then there was Fufu. Is it possible to find an aggressive bone in the body of a creature with a name like 'Fufu'? It would seem so. Surely only a rabbit could masquerade under such a name while c o m m i t t i n g u n s p e a k a b l e atrocities against poor, defenceless little field mice!

LITTLE RABBIT FUFU

Little rabbit Fufu
Hopping through the forest,
Scooping up the field mice
And bopping them on the
head!

Ridiculous-looking costumes worn by 'Bunny Girls' (although not everyone would agree here) hardly show respect for the rabbit although presumably they are intended to suggest cuteness and cuddliness. The outer image may appear to be soft and cuddly, but could there be something more sinister lurking behind this facade?

Perhaps our attitude to the rabbit has something to do with the reluctance with which we leave our childhood behind. As youngsters, we all loved him and found the cuddly toy version irresistible.

As adults, of course, we know better and have long ago found him out for what he really is: a pest, a nuisance.................... and he breeds like a .... well, like a rabbit.

Reaching sexual maturity in six months, the rabbit has about half a dozen litters a year, about half a dozen young in each litter and a life span of about ten years.

So under optimum conditions a pair of rabbits could well beget 300 young, each of which could beget 300 more per pair and so on and on and on. Before you could cry, "Ferret!" we could have an exponential nightmare on our hands!

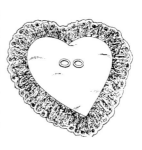

Such is the breeding success of this species that, far from being wiped out by disease, it has rewarded those families showing immunity or genetic resistance by allowing them to become the forefathers of whole new populations of super rabbits. And we all know the damage that can be done in our gardens by a super rabbit!

However, we persist in our love for this enigmatic creature. Why? Because we ourselves refuse to grow up? Perish the thought. But there's no denying the dilemma when, faced with yet another scene of devastation, we cry and tear our hair out, vowing to seek him out and kill him. Except there is always that wee small voice saying, "Ah.............".

Who knows the reason why we feel as we do? Let us just accept reality. The rabbit is here to stay, so our job is straightforward: **Enjoy the garden; enjoy the rabbit.**

2.
How to Garden with the Enemy

The first rule in gardening with the enemy is not to panic. From the list of plants given in chapters 4 & 5, choose mainly certainties so that you do not become discouraged. If you have been plagued by failures over the years, leaving you feeling pessimistic about the whole idea of having a full and varied garden, go straight out and buy a few reliable plants such as *aconitum*, mallow, lady's mantle, lavender and *mimulus*.

If you have had to resort to sowing a semi-wild garden, begin by reclaiming some areas close to the house, filling them with some real old die-hards. Risk one or two which just might survive the odd attack and if you do decide to plant some nice juicy treats, keep them safe overnight by adopting some of the methods described in chapter 10.

 Plan your layout as you would in a rabbit-free zone, selecting plants according to sun, shade, moisture, wind protection, etc. Remember to plan ahead, trying to imagine what your garden will look like in five years and ten years so that you allow space for growth. Fortunately there are enough specimens in the list to allow plenty of scope for the imaginative gardener.

To establish a sound basis to your scheme, select groups of rabbit-proof plants suitable for each area. Bear in mind you may wish to add others later by way of experiment. Combine tempting, ground level planting with generous clumps of perennials and evergreens, not forgetting height (trees, climbers) to frame the picture. Use containers not only for proven rabbit favourites which you want to keep out of reach, but also as a backup, planting one or two samples of anything which you fear may be lost. Once plants are established, you may propagate them to your heart's content. This is the stage when you know you have won and the victory is all the sweeter for being painless to all concerned.

Life being anything but simple, be prepared for the odd failure even among seemingly safe varieties. It is possible that local variations in rabbit habits have arisen due to natural selection in this fast-breeding species. Consequently you could step out one morning to discover to your horror that one or two specimens which are listed as being rabbit-proof have undergone the old familiar nocturnal metamorphosis which you know so well. Furthermore, some modern cultivars have been selected for traits such as colour or size. However, they may at the same time have lost a few genes which are unnecessary under ordinary circumstances but just happen to have made the original plant rabbit-proof. Such a disadvantage provides a good reason to keep on experimenting in order to find and grow as many 'safe' plants as possible.

Care should be taken with small, young plants which, although safe once they have grown, can be damaged by a rabbit out browsing to see what's new. You look around your plot to find decapitated *antirrhinum* or *aquilegia* which rabbits are not supposed to like! They don't eat them, but will occasionally bite bits off! Some overnight protection should take care of this irritating problem, as well as planting in sufficient numbers to withstand a bit of naughtiness.

Even *berberis thunbergii* will mysteriously lose some of its leaves when young despite being well armed with thorns. Just bear with the plant, protecting it through its first year and it should survive to a ripe old age without further protection.

Some plants, such as *spiraea*, seem to have a remarkable will to live so you can happily ignore the appearance of a 'shaved' area. However, if this lop-sided look does not appeal, it's time to resort to some overnight protection for the first few months (see chapter 10).

RULE #1

"'Tis a lesson you should heed,
Try, try again.
If at first you don't succeed,
Try, try again.

WILLIAM E. HICKSON

As success brings confidence, you may wish to add to the list more plants which you discover through trial and error. Always be prepared to try something new.

"Accuse not Nature,
She hath done her part;
Do thou but thine."

JOHN MILTON

14

3.
ALL SYSTEMS GO

Chapters 4 & 5 list eighty-one plants for mixing and matching according to individual conditions and personal taste. Use the list to inspire confidence and to kick-start your rabbit-free gardening career. Included in the list are:

(a) seven plants which rabbits mostly ignore but have been known to have the occasional nibble at in passing, especially if the plant is young and tender. This is just playfulness. He may simply snap off a flower head to give him something to do.

(b) seven plants which, although usually safe, include certain varieties that will be mercilessly devoured.

Although (a) and (b) can be included in your rabbit-proof scheme, special precautions may be taken to avoid encouraging such delinquent behaviour (see chapter 10). In chapter 5, these two groups have been indicated by:

(a) * vulnerable when young but otherwise safe;

(b) ** certain varieties are vulnerable.

Those awarded three stars *** have been tried and tested and thankfully appear to be completely ignored by the enemy. These are the wonderful specimens which should be purchased, planted and live a happy life no matter how many rabbits visit your garden.

Plants are listed in alphabetical order and, as well as the above rabbit-proof star rating, further information is included such as type of plant, conditions for growing, soil type etc. *Happy gardening!*

4.
A RABBIT-PROOF
A - B - C

This chapter provides a handy reference with rabbit-proof plants listed in alphabetical order. Space is provided so that names of new discoveries may be added.

The same plants are described again in detail in chapter 5 together with their rabbit-proof star rating. (See chapter 3 for more information on star ratings).

~~~~~~~~~~~~

*A*conitum napellus (**Monkshood**)
Alchemilla mollis (**Lady's Mantle**)
Anemone coronaria 'De Caen' (**Windflower**)
Antirrhinum majus (**Snapdragon**)
Aquilegia vulgaris (**Columbine, Granny's Bonnet**)
Aster novi-belgii (**Michaelmas Daisy**)
Aucuba japonica (**Spotted Laurel**)

*B*erberis darwinii (**Barberry**)
Berberis thunbergii 'Atropurpurea' (**Barberry**)
Bergenia cordifolia
Buddleja davidii (**Butterfly Bush**)
Buxus sempervirens (**Common Box**)

Calendula officinalis (**Marigold**)
Campanula medium (**Canterbury Bell**)
Chrysanthemum maximum (**Shasta Daisy**)
Ceanothus (**Californian Lilac**)
Ceanothus thyrsiflorus 'Repens'
Convollaria majalis (**Lily-of-the-Valley**)
Cornus (**Dogwood**)
Corydalis lutea
Cotoneaster
Crocosmia

Daphne
Dianthus barbatus (**Sweet William**)
Digitalis purpurea (**Common Foxglove**)
Doronicum plantagineum (**Leopard's Bane**)

Elaeagnus pungens
Endymion hispanicus (**Spanish Bluebell**)
Epenedium
Eucalyptus gunnii (**Cider Gum**)
Euphorbia (**Spurge / Milkweed**)

*G*alanthus nivalis (**Snowdrop**)
Geranium endressii (**Crane's Bill**)
Gladiolus

*H*edera helix (**Common Ivy**)
Helleborus lividus corsicus (**Corsican Hellebore**)
Hemerocallis (**Day Lily**)
Hosta (**Plantain Lily**)
Hydrangea macrophylla

*I*lex aquifolium (**Common Holly**)
Iris germanica (**Bearded Iris**)

*K*niphofia caulescens (**Red Hot Poker**)

*L*aburnum watereri 'Vossii' (**Golden Rain**)
Lavatera olbia (**Tree Mallow**)
Lavandula angustifolia (**Lavender**)
Lonicera japonica (**Japanese Honeysuckle**)
Lonicera periclymenum (**Honeysuckle / Woodbine**)
Lupinus (**Russell Lupin**)
Lychnis coronaria (**Campion**)

Malva moschata (**Musk Mallow**)
Meconopsis cambrica (**Welsh Poppy**)
Mimulus (**Monkey Flower**)
Monarda didyma (**Sweet Bergamot**)
Myosotis sylvatica (**Forget-me-not**)

Narcissus pseudonarcissus (**Wild Daffodil**)
Nepeta faassenii (**Catmint**)

Olearia macrodonta (**Daisy Bush**)

Paeonia officinalis (**Peony**)
Papaver orientalis (**Oriental Poppy**)
Papaver rhoeas (**Field Poppy**)
Philadelphus (**Mock Orange**)
Phormium tenax (**New Zealand Flax**)
Polygonatum (**Solomon's Seal**)
Polygonum affine / Persicaria affinis (**Knotweed**)
Potentilla (**Cinquefoil**)
Prunus laurucenasus (**Common Laurel**)

Rhododendron
Ribes sanguineum (**Flowering Currant**)
Rosa (**Rose**)
Rosmarinus (**Rosemary**)

Sambucus (**Elder**)
Skimmia japonica
Spirea japonica
Salvia superba
Sedum spectabile (**Ice Plant**)
Stachys byzantina olympus (**Lamb's Tongue**)
Syringa vulgaris (**Lilac**)

Trollius (**Globe Flower**)

Ulex europaeus (**Gorse**)

Viburnum tinus 'Laurustinus'
Viburnum opulus (**Guelder Rose**)
Vinca major (**Greater Periwinkle**)

LITTLE IDA'S FLOWERS

"Just then the door was suddenly opened, and a number of flowers danced in. Ida could not understand where these flowers came from, unless from the King's Garden. First came two lovely roses wearing golden crowns. These were the King and Queen.

Then followed stocks and pinks, bowing to all who were present. They had also a band with them. Great poppies and peonies blew upon the shells of peas till they were quite red in the face, whilst blue and white campanulas rang a merry peal on their bells. Then came a great many other flowers: violets, daisies, lilies of the valley, narcissus and others, who all moved so gracefully that it was delightful to see them."

HANS CHRISTIAN ANDERSEN

5.
RABBIT-PROOF PLANTS

key

P.	= Perennial		**rabbit-proof rating**
B.	= Biennial		
HA.	= Hardy annual	*	*Protect young*
S.	= Shrub		*plants*
C.	= Corm/bulb/tuber	**	*Certain varieties*
Cl.	= Climbing plant		*are vulnerable*
T.	= Tree	***	*Safe*

~~~~~~~~~~~~~~~~~~~~~~~~~~~~~~~

***Aconitum napellus (Monkshood)
P. Light shade; rich, moist soil. 5 foot high violet-blue flowers in July and August.

*Alchemilla mollis (Lady's Mantle)
P. Sun or light shade; ordinary soil. 12 inch high tiny green / yellow flowers amidst soft grey-green leaves from June to August.

*Anemone coronaria 'De Caen' (Windflower)
C. Warm, sheltered site; ordinary soil. 12 inch high brightly-coloured flowers throughout summer when planted throughout winter and spring.

***Antirrhinum majus (Snapdragon)
B. Full sun; well-drained, rich soil. 18 inch high spikes of bright colours from July to October.

22

****Aquilegia vulgaris (Columbine, Granny's Bonnet)**

P. Sun or light shade; moist, well-drained soil. 2 foot high stems with soft-coloured flowers above lush foliage, early summer. Leaves of some hybrids (e.g. Nora Barlow) are vulnerable to rabbits.

****Aster novi-belgii (Michaelmas Daisy)**

P. Full sun; fertile, moist, well-drained soil. 5 foot high pink / red / purple flowers with yellow centre, September to November. Avoid dwarf varieties.

*****Aucuba japonica (Spotted Laurel)**

S. Sun or shade; any soil. 6 foot high with narrow, bright green leaves bearing red berries in winter and spring.

*****Berberis darwinii (Barberry)**

S. Sun or light shade; well-drained soil. 8 foot high with bright orange blossom in Spring and holly-like berries in winter.

***Berberis thunbergii 'Atropurpurea' (Barberry)**

S. Sun; any soil. 4 foot high, thorny, spreading dark purple deciduous shrub. Leaves last throughout summer.

*	*Protect young plants*
**	*Certain varieties are vulnerable*
***	*Safe*

***Buddleja davidii* (Butterfly Bush)
S. Full sun, sheltered site; rich, well-drained soil. Tall, colours from pink to purple July to September.

***Buxus sempervirens* (Common Box)
S. Sun or shade; any soil. Can grow to 10 feet high and 6 feet wide if untrimmed. Evergreen.

***Calendula officinalis* (Marigold)
H.A. Sun. Any soil. 1 - 2 foot high yellow or orange flowers throughout summer.

Campanula medium (Canterbury Bell)
B. Sun or light shade; well-drained soil. 1 - 3 foot high with white, pink or blue flowers May to July.

***Cornus* (Dogwood)
S. Sun or light shade; moist soil. Over 6 foot high. Deciduous with attractive stems in winter.

***Ceanothus* (Californian Lilac)
S. Full sun in sheltered site; well-drained, neutral soil. Dense, glossy foliage reaches 10 foot high with small blue flowers in late spring.

***Ceanothus thyrsiflorus* 'Repens'
S. Full sun in sheltered site; well-drained, neutral or alkaline soil. Up to 3 foot high, ground-covering shrub smothers weeds with blue flowers in May which continue smoky-blue throughout autumn.

Chrysanthemum maximum (Shasta Daisy)

P. Sun or partial shade; rich, well-drained, moist soil. White blooms with yellow centres from June to September.

***Convollaria majalis* (Lily-of-the-Valley)

P. Sun or light shade; any soil. 9 inch high fast-growing plant with sweetly-scented white flowers in late spring.

***Corydalis lutea*

P. Light shade; good drainage essential. 2 foot high yellow flowers with grey-green leaves, colonising cracks in walls and paving in shady sites. Flowers April to November.

***Cotoneaster*

S. Full sun; well-drained soil. Ground cover or bushy (depending on variety) bearing small flowers in early summer and berries in autumn.

***Crocosmia*

C. Sun; ordinary soil. 2 - 3 foot high spikes bearing orange flowers amid strong, narrow leaves from July to September.

*　　*Protect young plants*
**　　*Certain varieties are vulnerable*
***　*Safe*

Daphne
S. Sun or light shade; well-drained, moist soil. Between 2 and 5 feet (depending on variety). Fast-growing *D. Burkwoodii* bears soft pink, scented flowers early summer and also in autumn.

***Dianthus barbatus* (Sweet William)**
B. Full sun; well-drained soil. 1 - 2 foot high red, pink or white scented flowers in summer above evergreen foliage.

***Digitalis purpurea* (Common Foxglove)**
B. Sun or shade; well-drained, moist soil. Up to 5 foot high stems of bell-shaped white, pink or purple flowers above soft foliage in June and July.

Doronicum plantagineum* (Leopard's Bane)
P. Sun or light shade; moist soil. 2 foot high clumps of bright green leaves with yellow daisies in early spring.

****Elaeagnus pungens 'maculata'***
S. Sun or light shade; ordinary soil. 10 foot high evergreen with creamy-yellow markings on leaves.

***Endymion hispanicus* (Spanish Bluebell)**
C. Semi-shade; moist, well-drained soil. 12 inch high stems bearing blue bells above glossy foliage from April to June.

Epenedium
P. Light shade; ordinary fertile soil. 12 inch high ground-cover of bronze then green heart-shaped foliage with red and white blooms in early spring.

Eucalyptus gunnii (Cider Gum)
T. Full sun; moist, well-drained, acid or neutral soil. Evergreen with rounded, silvery leaves when young, turning to pointed, dark green / bluish when mature.

**Euphorbia* (Spurge/Milkweed)
P. Sun or partial shade; ordinary soil. 18 inch high clumps of pale leaves topped with greenish-yellow flowers in late spring.

Galanthus nivalis (Snowdrop)
C. Shade; retentive soil. 8 inch high green-tipped white flowers in late winter.

**Geranium endressii* (Crane's Bill)
P. Sun or light shade; well-drained soil. 12 - 18 inch high spreading plant with pink flowers throughout Summer. Many varieties of geranium. 'Johnson's Blue' survives the rabbit while white varieties seem to attract nibblers.

*   *Protect young plants*
**   *Certain varieties are vulnerable*
***   *Safe*

27

Gladiolus
C. Full sun; fertile, well-drained soil. 3 - 4 feet high colourful flower heads amidst sword-shaped foliage.

Hedera helix (Common Ivy)
Cl. Sun or shade; ordinary soil. Self-supporting evergreen swarming over ground, fences and walls.

Helleborus lividus corsicus (Corsican Hellebore)
P. Sun or shade; any soil. 2 foot high yellow-green flower heads above leathery green foliage from winter to spring.

Hemerocallis (Day Lily)
P. Sun or light shade; ordinary soil. 2 foot high scented yellow flowers in early summer.

Hosta (Plantain Lily)
P. Light shade; moist soil. Up to 2 feet high with large, veined leaves.

Hydrangea macrophylla
S. Dappled shade; moist, fertile soil. 5 foot high with pink (in alkaline soil) or blue (in acid soil) flower heads throughout summer.

Ilex aquifolium (Common Holly)
T. Sun or shade; well-drained soil. Slow-growing evergreen with red berries borne on the female plant in winter.

***Iris germanica* (Bearded Iris)
C. Full sun; fertile soil. 2 - 3 foot high with purple flowers amidst clumps of grassy leaves in early summer. Many varieties of differing colours.

***Kniphofia caulescens* (Red Hot Poker)
P. Full sun; well-drained soil. 2 foot high stems bearing red - yellow spikes in Autumn amidst clumps of evergreen leaves.

***Laburnum watereri 'Vossii'* (Golden Rain)
T. Sun or light shade; well-drained, moist soil. 15 - 20 foot high with long racemes of yellow flowers in early summer.

***Lavatera olbia* (Tree Mallow)
S. Full sun; well-drained soil. 6 - 8 foot high with pink flowers from June to November.

***Lavandula angustifolia* (Lavender)
P. Sun; well-drained soil. 2 foot high spikes of heavily scented silver-grey foliage and lavender flowers.

***Lonicera japonica* (Japanese Honeysuckle)
Cl. Full sun or light shade; rich, retentive soil. Evergreen, climbing to 20 feet with white to yellow scented flowers.

*	*Protect young plants*
**	*Certain varieties are vulnerable*
***	*Safe*

***Lonicera periclymenum** (Honeysuckle/Woodbine)

P. Full sun or light shade; rich, retentive soil. 15 - 20 feet with deliciously scented purple-tinged, creamy flowers.

Lupinus (Russell Lupin)

P. Sun; retentive soil. 3 - 4 foot high spikes of blooms in varying shades from white to purple. Young dwarf varieties will be stripped of their foliage unless protected.

***Lychnis coronaria** (Campion)

P. Sun or light shade; ordinary soil. 1 foot high with soft, grey, downy foliage and red flowers in early summer.

***Malva moschata** (Musk Mallow)

P. Sun or light shade; well-drained soil. 3 foot high with masses of pink flowers throughout summer.

***Meconopsis cambrica** (Welsh Poppy)

P. Sun or shade. Any soil. 12 inches high with delicate orange or yellow blooms throughout summer.

***Mimulus** (Monkey Flower)

B. Partial shade; moist, retentive soil. 12 inches high, flowering from July until October.

***Monarda didyma* (Sweet Bergamot)
P. Sun; moist, retentive soil. 3 foot high hooded, aromatic flowers of red or pink from June to September.

***Myosotis sylvatica* (Forget-me-not)
B. Partial shade; fertile, moist soil. 6 - 15 inch high with tiny blue flowers, April until June.

***Narcissus pseudonarcissus* (Wild Daffodil)
C. Sun; well-drained soil. 12 - 18 inch high yellow trumpets amidst narrow foliage.

***Nepeta faassenii* (Catmint)
P. Sun; well-drained soil. 12 - 18 inch high greyish leaves with blue/lavender flowers in summer.

***Olearia macrodonta* (Daisy Bush)
S. Full sun; well-drained soil. Reaches 8 foot high, with glossy grey-green leaves and clusters of small scented flowers in summer.

***Paeonia officinalis* (Peony)
P. Full sun; retentive soil. 2 foot high with attractive foliage and large crimson blooms in May or June.

*	*Protect young plants*
**	*Certain varieties are vulnerable*
***	*Safe*

***Papaver orientalis* (Oriental Poppy)
P. Full sun; ordinary soil. 2 - 3 foot high scarlet (or pink or white) blooms with striking black centres.

***Papaver rhoeas* (Field Poppy)
H.A. Sun; well-drained soil. Up to 2 foot high scarlet, white or pink delicate blooms.

***Philadelphus* (Mock Orange)
S. Sun; any soil. 3 - 8 foot high with orange-perfumed white flowers in early summer.

***Phormium tenax* (New Zealand Flax)
S. Full sun or partial shade; fertile soil. Up to 8 foot high vertical leaves. Evergreen.

***Polygonatum* (Solomon's Seal)
P. Light shade; fertile soil. 2 - 4 foot long stems with curved leaves and hung with white, bell-shaped flowers in June.

***Polygonum affine / Persicaria affinis* (Knotweed)
P. Light shade; fertile, retentive soil. 6 - 9 inch high, ground cover with pink spiked blooms in autumn when leaves turn reddish-bronze.

**Potentilla* (Cinquefoil)
S. Full sun or light shade; any soil. 3 - 4 foot high with small leaves and abundant flowers, early summer until late autumn.

Avoid *P. nepalensis* and *P. atrosanguinea.*

***Prunus laurocenasus* (Common Laurel)
S. Shade; alkaline soil. Up to 15 feet high evergreen with dense shiny leaves and white flower spikes in April followed by red berries.

***Rhododendron*
S. Light shade; moist, acid soil. Many varieties (incl. Azalea) from dwarf to 60 foot high. Most species flower in May and June; some in spring or autumn.

***Ribes sanguineum* (Flowering Currant)
S. Sun or light shade. 10 foot high evergreen with creamy-yellow markings on leaves.

**Rosa* (Rose)
P./S./Cl. Most roses will be left in peace by the rabbit. Protect young rambling roses and avoid planting patio roses.

***Rosmarinus* (Rosemary)
S. Full sun; well-drained soil. Up to 6 foot high with narrow, aromatic leaves and grey-blue flowers in late spring and early summer.

***Sambucus* (Elder)
S. Sun or light shade; rich, moist soil. 8 foot high with white flowers in April and scarlet berries in autumn.

*	*Protect young plants*
**	*Certain varieties are vulnerable*
***	*Safe*

*Skimmia japonica

S. Sun or light shade; ordinary soil. 5 foot high evergreen leaves with orange scent when crushed. Fragrant white flowers in April and May; red berries on female plant in September.

**Spiraea japonica

S. Full sun; ordinary soil. 3 - 5 foot high narrow-leafed shrub with heads of tiny pink flowers in late summer. Dwarf varieties (e.g. *Alpina*) are nibbled when young but should survive.

***Salvia superba

P. Full sun; ordinary soil. 3 foot high deep purple flowers from July to September.

***Sedum spectabile (Ice Plant)

P. Sun; well-drained soil. 18 inch high thick, fleshy leaves with large heads of deep pink flowers in late summer.

***Stachys byzantina 'Olympus' (Lamb's Tongue)

P. Full sun; ordinary soil. Fleecy, silvery ground-covering leaves with 18 inch high spires bearing small purple flowers in early summer.

***Syringa vulgaris (Lilac)

S. Sun; well-drained soil. 12 foot high with white, scented flowers in May and June.

Trollius (Globe Flower)
P. Full sun or very light shade; fertile, moist soil. Over 2 foot high with bright green leaves and large, orange or yellow flowers.

Ulex europaeus (Gorse)
S. Full sun; tolerates poor, dry soil. Tall, thorny bush with small golden flowers in spring.

Viburnum tinus 'Laurustinus'
S. Partial shade; moist soil. 4 - 5 foot high dark, glossy-leaved evergreen with white flowers through winter to spring.

Viburnum opulus (Guelder Rose)
S. Partial shade; moist soil. Up to 12 inch high, this deciduous bush has white flowers in May and June and red berries in autumn, when its leaves turn red.

Vinca major 'Elegantissima' (Greater Periwinkle)
S. Shade; well-drained, moist soil. Hardy evergreen ground cover with cream-bordered green leaves bearing blue flowers from April to June.

~~~~~~~~~~~~~~~~~~~~~~~

key

P.	= Perennial		*rabbit-proof rating*
B.	= Biennial		
HA.	= Hardy annual	*	*Protect young*
S.	= Shrub		*plants*
C.	= Corm/bulb/tuber	**	*Certain varieties*
Cl.	= Climbing plant		*are vulnerable*
T.	= Tree	***	*Safe*

THE GARDEN OF PARADISE

The rocks above them grew like mists, and at last were as clear and bright as white clouds in the moonlight. The air was balmy, fresh as a breeze among the mountains, and fragrant as one blowing through a valley of roses. A river, as clear as the air itself, flowed at their feet. Gold and silver fish swam in it; purple eels, that emitted blue sparks at every motion, were playing beneath its surface, and the broad leaves of the water-lilies that floated upon it shone with all the colours of the rainbow.

The glowing orange-coloured flower itself seemed to draw its nourishment from the water, as the flame of a lamp draws its nourishment from the oil. A bridge of marble, of such cunning workmanship that it seemed made of lace and pearl, led over the water to the Island of Bliss, where bloomed the Garden of Paradise.

HANS CHRISTIAN ANDERSEN

6.
WHAT MAKES A PLANT RABBIT-PROOF?

Think what you will about the rabbit, you have to admit he has left us with quite a selection of every height and habit to choose from: perennials, shrubs, bulbs, even some biennials and hardy annuals. But just why he seems to find these plants unpalatable remains something of a mystery.

To call a plant 'rabbit-proof' may be to tempt fate and it has been observed that no rabbit has yet read the list! As a general rule, they tend to avoid plants which are scented, tough, thorny or poisonous, but this fails to explain their aversion to many of the above plants. If only the rules governing rabbits' tastes were this easy! Rabbits do indeed like some scented flowers (for example, sweet pea). Why, if they don't eat wild daisies, will they devour Bellis daisies? If not certain roses, why the patio rose? If not the old Russell lupins, why some of the new ones?

Perhaps one day we will know just what exactly repels a rabbit. We could speculate until the cows come home, but for now all we have to go on is empirical evidence. No matter. Follow the example of the old cottagers: if it grows, grow it. Presumably it is no coincidence that many traditional 'cottage' plants remain uneaten.

SONNET

From you I have been absent in the spring,
When proud-pied April, dress'd in all his trim,
Hath put a spirit of youth in every thing,
That heavy Saturn laugh'd and leap'd with him.
Yet nor the lay of birds, nor the sweet smell
Of different flowers in odour and in hue,
Could make me any summer's story tell,
Or from their proud lap pluck them where they
grew:
Nor did I wonder at the lily's white,
Nor praise the deep vermilion in the rose;
They were but sweet, but figures of delight,
Drawn after you, you pattern of all those.
　　Yet seem'd it winter still, and, you away,
　　As with your shadow I with these did play.

WILLIAM SHAKESPEARE

7.
CHANGE WITH THE SEASONS

Celebrate the early part of the year with a display of snowdrops followed by daffodils, bluebells and forget-me-nots. The latter can be planted amid yellow Welsh poppies. Grow *ceanothus* in the sun and site Russell lupins behind wild poppies as well as some well-placed clumps of iris.

A generous planting of *aconitum, lavatera* and musk mallow will take you through the summer, lifting your spirits. Add *aquilegia,* lavender and lady's mantle with some mature *berberis* for contrast. *Potentilla* shrubs are wonderful, but avoid the succulent varieties. The choice is endless for this season.

For a sound backdrop to your blooms, you can rely on holly, ivy, box and *cotoneaster.* If you have space, include *buddleja,* laurel, honeysuckle, rhododendron, azaleas, lilac and *hydrangea.* Sail towards the later part of summer into autumn with the long-lasting *mimulus* (also good for pots) at the front of a border and the addition of the striking *monarda* in a sunny spot.

Michaelmas daisies and *crocosmia* help maintain a splash of colour through the changing of the clock while *viburnum* is an absolute 'must' to herald in winter.

8.
THE ZERO OPTION

As well as knowing what can be grown, it makes sense to know what to avoid trying to grow. There is absolutely no point in wasting time and money on delicious, juicy plants if you live in a rabbit-infested area, unless you are sure they can be protected.

Most annuals taste delicious to a rabbit. Overnight, a beautiful bed of young plants can just disappear, leaving you with nothing but useless green stumps to weep over. This list contains some of our best-loved flowers as well as a few lesser-known examples and should be endless. You may well have discovered the hard way many more to add to this list!

~~~~~~~~~~~~~~~~~~~~~~

EXAMPLES OF PLANTS THAT RABBITS EAT

Achillea; Alyssum; Astilbe; Bellis daisy; Busy Lizzie; Centranthus; Chrysanthemum; Crocus; Dahlia; Delphinium; Fuchsia; Gaillardia; Godetia; Grape hyacinth; Lobelia erinus; Marguerite; Nasturtium; Ornamental cabbage; Pansy; Patio Rose; Petunia; Potentilla atrosanguinea; Potentilla nepalensis; Primula; Sweet Pea; Viola; Viola Labradorica; Zonal Pelargonium.

9.
THE VIOLENT OPTION

This book is all about learning how to co-exist with the rabbit. Gardeners are on the whole really nice people who cannot bear the thought of taking up arms against the enemy.

"Come out of there, you ruinous wretch!"

If you follow the advice given, you should not even have to give this course of action a second thought.

"There never was a good war or a bad peace."

BENJAMIN FRANKLIN

10.
THE STUBBORN GARDENERS' OPTIONS

If, like most people, you still prefer to grow some favourites despite the determination of Mr. Rabbit to fill his belly with them, here are a dozen ideas (most of which have been suggested by experienced gardeners) which should make life difficult for him. They are not all fool-proof, but you may wish to experiment for yourself.

Precautionary notes are included, so you know what to expect.

A. CREOSOTE-SOAKED STRING

Encircle your flower bed with string tied around short posts to a height of 4 inches (10 cm) above ground level. Periodically soak string with creosote.

This deterrent has two obvious drawbacks:
(a) creosote is a wonderful weedkiller, ensuring that you lose your plant anyway if it comes into contact with the leaves;
(b) rainfall or watering lead to contamination of the soil and subsequent long-term damage.

B. EPSOM SALTS

Epsom salts sprinkled around your plant should discourage the rabbit for a while.

Rain or watering will dissolve the salts.

C. NEWSPAPERS IN THE RABBIT HOLE

 Stuff newspaper into the rabbit hole, thus irritating Mr. Bunny and encouraging him to go elsewhere. It seems he doesn't like the rustling noise of the paper.

Rabbits can travel. You may fool some of the rabbits some of the time.............................

D. HELIUM-FILLED BALLOONS

This idea has been suggested as a deterrent to hungry grey squirrels, but might be worth a try if you don't mind your garden looking like a fairground. Tie the balloon firmly to a stake in the ground.

E. PROTECTION FOR INDIVIDUAL SMALL PLANTS

Rinse out an empty plastic bottle (2 or 3 litre) and cut off the top 4 inches (10 cm). Pierce holes in both the top part and the bottom part and use as a small cloche to protect individual plants overnight.

Rather fussy, but very effective.

F. PROTECTION FOR INDIVIDUAL LARGE PLANTS

In addition to tough plastic tree protectors which can be bought, you can also make your own version. Staple each end of a length of wire mesh to a cane, leaving a few inches of the cane protruding from the bottom. You may also line the wire mesh with polythene attached at intervals by a short piece of string. Encircle the plant with the wire mesh and insert the canes into the ground.

Not pretty to look at; time-consuming to fit and remove. This option is nevertheless a handy compromise between a large, expensive fence and no fence at all.

G. ULTRASOUND

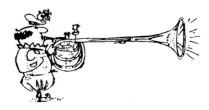

Rabbits and other small animals can hear sounds in the 18 to 15.5 kilohertz range which is beyond that of most humans. An electronic device which emits a high frequency ultrasound beam is placed in your garden, annoying the rabbit and sending him smartly on his way.

Fortunately, birds are unaffected by this device. However, other small animals such as cats (themselves useful rabbit deterrents) which you may welcome into your garden will not thank you for resorting to this option. Rabbits have been known to enter the garden backwards, thus shielding their ears from the sound. Some have even invited their friends around to experience the 'buzz' for themselves!

H. THE OLD FAITHFUL FENCE

A favourite method of keeping rabbits out of your garden is to surround the whole area with a four foot high fence buried to a depth of one to two feet (30/60 cm). This is certainly effective and the idea comes into its own when used around a nursery bed (even a wire mesh here) where young plants can be molly-coddled until they are large, fibrous and better able to survive the enemy.

This excellent option is rather expensive and its success depends on the gate being kept closed (see foreword).

J. THE BLACK THREAD THREAT

Make a 'cat's cradle' of black thread, entwined around natural twigs which you insert into the ground to form an exclusion zone around a favourite small plant. The rabbit feels the thread, but cannot see it and so it acts as an invisible threat.

Reports on the reliability of this method vary, although it certainly seems to deter cats. Rather fiddly to construct, but cheap and worth a try. Birds may become entangled.

K. THE SNEAKY OPTION

This is almost too obvious to mention and (necessity being the mother of invention) most people will already have discovered the sneaky option for themselves.

If you want to drive your enemy to distraction, simply fill a few containers with the most delicious of blooms (nasturtiums, violas, marguerites etc.) and place them on an auricula theatre or hang them on the wall. Then sit back and smile.

Similar satisfaction comes from a well-stocked flower tower or hanging basket. If you have containers on the ground, just lift them to the bench in the evening.

Good news if you like seasonal splashes of colour: this option has no obvious drawbacks.

L. THE MEDICINAL OPTION

Take a bottle of castor oil, add some paprika, mustard powder and ground pepper. Shake vigorously, enjoying the illusion that you are grasping a rabbit's neck. Sprinkle medicine over vulnerable plants. *Temporary.*

M. LION DUNG

Clay pellets impregnated with liquidised lion dung and spread around flower borders will frighten rabbits away, since the lion (being of a predatory nature) also excretes a phenol compound to mark his scent.

Pellets are irradiated, therefore disease-free and ecologically safe. Also very effective at chasing off badgers, squirrels and deer.

N. THE UNSPEAKABLE OPTION

........................unthinkable!

P. THE SENSIBLE RABBIT'S OWN OPTION

Eventually the rabbit will feel he has no choice but to adapt to his food-free environment and go off to seek his fortunes in a new profession. After all, there are plenty of options open to the sensible rabbit, none of which would do his 'cute' image any harm at all.

Easter Bunny,
Conjurer's Assistant,
Bunny Girl,
Carrot Juice Manufacturer,
Landscape Gardener................

Dream on.............................

portrait of a
sensible rabbit

11.
THE FIGHT IS OVER

Chapter 10 should have provided a few weapons for your anti-rabbit armoury should they be needed. However, it is to be hoped you will discover the freedom of growing plants which can simply be a joy to look at rather than a source of anxiety.

Once you notice all the butterflies and bees thronging around your wonderful blooms again, you will know the battle has been won. Then you can relax and remember the dreams you had when you first began to create a garden. Lazy, hazy days can at last be what they were meant to be.

Moreover, you can look
forward with a
clear conscience
to guilt-free
as well as stress-free
gardening.
You are happy,
your plants are happy,
the rabbit is happy,
everything is happy.
What more could
any gardener
wish for?

*   *   *

THE END

INDEX OF TOPICS

INDEX OF EXTRACTS & ILLUSTRATIONS

SEED TIME AND HARVEST

My hollyhocks are all awake.
And not a single rose is lost;
My wallflowers, for dear pity's sake,
Have fought the winter's cruel frost;
Pink peony buds begin to peer,
And flags push up their sword blades fine:
I know there will not be this year
A brighter garden plot than mine.

I'll sow the seeds of mignonette,
Of snapdragon and sunflowers tall,
And scarlet poppies I will set
To flower against the southern wall;
Already all my lilies show
The green crowns baby lilies wear,
And all my flowers will grow and blow,
Because Love's hand hath set them there.

I'll plant and water, sow and weed,
Till not an inch of earth shows brown,
And take a vow of each small seed
To grow to greenness and renown:
And then some day you'll pass my way,
See gold and crimson, bell and star,
And catch my garden's soul and say:-
'How sweet these cottage gardens are!'

E. NESBIT

54

ACKNOWLEDGEMENTS

This guide has been a pleasure to compile not least since it has led to many an entertaining conversation!

I would like to thank everyone involved for offering advice and for willingly discussing ideas. For advice and inspiration, my gratitude to Stanley Thomson, Alison Muir, Anne Cameron and Caroline Walton; *for expert gardening advice,* Alyson Dorrington; W.S. Dunbar, Elmwood Nurseries, Symington; W. Forrest, Headspoint Nurseries, Carluke; and Iris Gray (Beechgrove Garden), Tern Television; *and for technical assistance and equipment,* Clyde Computer Centre, Glasgow and GEF Printers, Glasgow.

My thanks also to Mum and Dad for keeping the garden alive through years of rabbit occupation.

J.T.

STOP PRESS.......

Reports are coming in of emaciated rabbits seen wandering dazed, hungry and in search of food in gardens across the country.

Do not be fooled by this behaviour. A few old cabbage leaves tossed into the compost heap will do the trick.

Then simply retire gracefully, looking the other way at all times.

*   *   *

MORE
RABBIT-PROOF PLANTS

This further list of 51 plants has been compiled thanks to readers' responses to 'Gardening with the Enemy'. In addition, it appears that most herbs are ignored by rabbits (e.g. chives, fennel, mint, oregano, sage and thyme). Vegetable growers should construct well-protected plots (see page 44) or experiment with companion planting, growing 'safe bets' such as marigolds, parsley, teucrium or curry plant amongst the goodies. On a happy note, though rabbits will nibble runner beans they seem to shy away from broad beans!

key

A.	= Annual
C.	= Corm/bulb/tuber
H.	= Herb/grass
P.	= Perennial
R.	= Rock Plant
S.	= Shrub

* Protect young plants

~~~~~~~~~~~~~~~~~~~~~~~~~~~~~~~~~~~~

*A*canthus spinosus **(Bear's Breeches)**	P.
Ajuga reptans **(Bugle)**	P.
Anaphalis cinnamomea **(syn. A. yedoensis)**	P.
Arundinana	P.
Astrantia major **(Masterwort)**	P.
B*egonia *tuberosa* **(Tuberous Begonia)	C.
Brunnera macrophylla **(Siberian Bugloss)**	R.
*C*amomile	H.
Centaurea montana **(Mountain Knapweed)**	P.
Choisya ternata **(Mexican Orange)**	S.
Cistus purpureus **(Rock Rose)**	S.
Curry Plant	H.
* Cytisus scoparius **(Common Broom)**	S.
D*ahlia hortensis **(Dahlia)	C.
Dianthus **(Pinks)**	A.

*E*chinops ritro **(Globe Thistle***)*   P.
Echium lycopsis **(Borage)**   A.
Eringium **(Sea Holly)**   P.

*F*atsia japonica   S.
Fuchsia **(Hardy Shrub Fuchsia)**   S.

G*eranium **(all perennial varieties)   P.
Geum borisii **(Avens)**   P.

*H*ebe pinguifolia **(Veronica)**   S.
Heuchera sanguinea **(Coral Flower)**   P.
Hellebore **(all types)**   P.
Hypericum **(St. John's Wort)**   S.
Hyacinthus orientalis **(Dutch Hyacinth)**   C.

*I*beris umbellata **(Candytuft)**   A.
Iris xiphioides **(Dutch/English Iris)**   C.

*L*aurus nobilis **(Sweet Bay)**   S.
Lilium 'Shuksan' **(Bellingham Hybrid)**   C.
Lychnis chalcedonica **(Campion, Maltese Cross)** P.
Lysimachia punctata **(Yellow Loosestrife)**   P.
Lythrum salicaria Robert **(Purple Loosestrife)** P.

*M*econopsis betonicifolia **(Himalayan Blue Poppy)** P.

*N*icotiana alata **(Tobacco Plant)**   A.

*O*enothera missouriensis **(Evening Primrose)**   P.

*P*hlox paniculata   P.

* Primula vulgaris (**Primrose**)   P.
Pulmonaria saccharata (**Lungwort**)   P.

***R**anunculus aconitifolius* (**Batchelors' Buttons**)   P.
Rodgersia aesculifolia   P.
Ruta graveolens (**Rue**)   S.

***S**alix reticulata* (**Net-leaved Willow**)   R.
Saxifraga umbrosa (**London Pride**)   R.
Saxifraga longifolia (**Tumbling Waters**)   R.
Sidalcea malviflora   P.
Solidago (**Golden Rod**)   P.

***T**eucrium hermanicum* (**Wall Germander**)   R.

***Y**ucca gloriosa* (**Spanish Dagger**)   P.

READERS' LETTERS

'I am absolutely besieged with rabbits and have a Surrey friend who also complains of her garden looking like Colditz! If you do have any copies still for sale, please could you send me two of them?

    'We run to extra athletic bunnies here... One raider has been getting into my triple-fenced vegetable garden recently, but I gave chase a couple of nights ago. Before my astonished eyes it took a flying leap over the two-and-a-half-foot wire netting and straight through between two stakes of the outer chestnut paling! You have to admire such determination!' Mrs. Macdonald, Ross-shire.

*

'Please rush me a copy of your book as I too am plagued by the spawn of Satan - rabbits!?

    '...... If all else fails, I can always throw the book at the little sods.' Mr. Burton, Jersey.

First published in Scotland in 1996 by

JANET THOMSON
5 Circus Place
Glasgow G31 2JJ
Scotland
www.rabbitgarden.com

First edition November 1996
Second edition January 1997
Third edition August 1998
Fourth Edition June 2001
Fifth Edition October 2002

ISBN 0-9530013-0-X

9 780953 001309

Published on SMS multi-media computer supplied by
Clyde Computer Centre, Unit A4, Fullarton Road, Glasgow G32 8YL
www.GlasgowComputing.com

Published in Glasgow
Compiled by *GEF Printers, 2 Camlachie Street, Glasgow G31 4JH*

* * *